We Time
Derek Triplett

We Time"
by Derek Triplett
© 2018 by Derek Triplett

For information, address:
Derek Triplett – derektriplett.com
International Standard Book Number: 978-0-9997556-0-0

Library of Congress Catalogue Card Number: Available Upon Request

Printed in the United States of America First Edition, Jan, 2018

Trademarks

Contact the Author
Connect with Derek Triplett at
booking@derektriplett.com
Visit his Website at
www.derektriplett.com
Derek Triplett
dtrip@derektriplett.com

Dedication

I dedicate this book to every person who regrets the fact that a love relationship failed because at the time you did not have the tools to make it work and to every couple who will use this book as a resource to help make their love last.

Special Thanks

To my family for your love and support
To the 3D Trip team for your commitment and devotion
To Byrdology for partnering with my vision and enhancing it with your knowledge and creativity

You are friends, lovers, and partners. Build each aspect of the relationship.

Think about it.

You are committed to each other. Your connection has different layers. You have several functions, playing multiple roles each one having to be nurtured and executed. Talk and share with each other as friends. Give that best friend support. Don't let the other responsibilities of marriage and family life take a toll on your love life. Be romantic, sensual and sexual on a regular basis. Keep your team dynamics in good condition. Each of you is one part of a powerful whole. Like Batman and Robin, peanut butter and jelly, Lucy and Ricky, Stockton and Malone, you two are partners.

Pray this together

God in heaven, thank you for the wonderful person with whom I am sharing my life. Please continue to make us one. It is my desire to be an excellent partner, lover and friend. Help us to fulfill each other in every aspect of our lives. Let our commitment and connection to each other make us even better individuals. We love each other and want the best relationship possible. Amen.

Do this together

Find something this week to do as friends. In addition, do a tandem exercise. Be partners in a board or card game or work on a project together where both of you have a contribution to make. Lastly, married people, talk about ways to enhance your love life and then go get it in.

Notes

Daily take your relationship to God in prayer. Pray for your partner. Pray for yourself. Pray for specific aspects of the relationship. Some things only happen in relationships through the power of love and the power of God.

Think about it.

Trust me, you want God's involvement in your relationship. All couples want God to bless their union, but His blessing can be tied to how much He is allowed to participate in the relationship. Make it a habit to enlist God's assistance in your partnership. Your relationship and the two of you will be the better for it. He is the originator of unconditional love. We all need his help to even come close to that quality of love.

Pray this together

God in heaven, you hear and answer prayer. I pray that my partner in love and life would also be my prayer partner for this relationship. As we daily place our love on the altar, we ask for your divine assistance. Empower each of us to be the ideal mate. Help us during the tough times that we might grow through them, and protect us from any evil influences that seek to destroy our union. We love each other and want the best relationship possible. Amen.

Do this together

Set aside specific times to jointly pray for your relationship. Prayer is one of the most intimate things two people can do together.

Notes

Never allow yourself to view your mate as an opponent even in an ongoing dispute. Fight for the relationship even when you're fighting with each other. Stay in each other's corner.

Think about it.

Conflicts are inevitable. How you handle them and how you regulate yourselves during them will determine if they become damaging to your relationship. Never go in for the kill. Your partner should never be the enemy you are determined to defeat. Your goal is resolution and reconciliation. Effectively manage any hurt feelings, pain and anger and remember you are in a dispute with the love of your life who is just temporarily getting on your nerves.

Pray this together

God in heaven, you are the God of peace and not the author of confusion. We understand that we will not always agree. We will make mistakes or bad choices that may cause each other pain. We ask that your spirit would help us conquer any negative emotions that happen during conflict. We pray for the will to continue to communicate openly and honestly and to seek every means of peaceful resolution of any conflict we may have. We pray that we would treat each other with honor and respect regardless of the circumstances. We love each other and want the best relationship possible. Amen.

Do this together

Each of you discuss how best to engage you during conflict. Set some parameters with language and physicality. Articulate what is out of bounds during arguments and fights. Pre-set guidelines give you a better chance of maintaining appropriate behavior when emotionally charged.

Notes

/04

When you determine who you love, decide to make it known on a daily basis.

Think about it.

Love is deliberate. When you decide to love, you become very intentional. As time goes on you may need to discipline yourselves to consistently express your love to each other. Use what you know about your partner's love language to daily communicate love in an unmistakable manner. Knowing you are loved is a great way spend each day.

Pray this together

God in heaven, you so loved the world that you gave your son to die for our sins. Teach us to love like you and daily express it to each other. Help us to overcome any personality traits that would hinder our ability to show love to each other. Deliver us from any past damage that would make it difficult for us to receive love. We pray for the best relationship possible. Amen.

Do this together

Have a conversation about how you most like to give and receive love. List your top 2 or 3 favorite love songs and talk about why they are your favorite. Listen to them together. Feel free to dance.

Notes

Real love never just goes away. It lives or it dies. You help it to live. You help it to die.

Think about it.

Each partner is required to do his or her part to maintain the love relationship. I cannot stress this enough. Either love will blossom because it receives the requisite attention or it will potentially die because of neglect. No matter how good your relationship is, continue to do what is necessary to maintain it like a farmer tends to his crops. Do not wait on attention to be given and then give it in return. Take the initiative and be prepared for your partner to reciprocate.

Pray this together

God in heaven, you give us life along with the desire and the capacity to love. We have a special love that neither of us should ever ignore. We pray that we never take each other for granted and that you would cause us to do those things that help our love to remain alive and our relationship to grow. Let me not do anything to destroy the love we have. We desire the best relationship possible. Amen.

Do this together

Go down memory lane. Discuss the highlights of your relationship. Rehearse the special moments.

Notes

Love is birthed. Love breathes. Love grows. Love feeds. Love hurts. Love bleeds. Love is bandaged. Love heals. Love lives.

Think about it.

Forever is such a poetic word. My definition of forever is every day until you die. It is not poetic, but it is accurate. If you plan to be together forever your relationship will go through changes, ups and downs, highs, and lows. Commit to the end you hoped for at the beginning. Try not to get overwhelmed by any particular difficult period. Work on your love, and work with your lover to your last breath. Do not forfeit your happy ending by giving up too soon. Again, remain committed to the end you hoped for at the beginning.

Pray this together

God in heaven, you are the everlasting God. We pray that our love would last. We pray that we would always remember to be thankful for the good times and celebrate them accordingly. Give us the strength to endure the rough times and face every test with wisdom, tenacity and patience. With your help, we can live happily ever after. We pray that together we will make that dream a reality. We love each other and want the best relationship possible. Amen.

Do this together

Find a couple who has been happily married for 30 years or more and have a conversation with them. Ask them about their life together and the secrets of their longevity. If you have been married for that length of time, find a new couple and share your story.

Notes

Relationships are a risk. Vulnerability is a necessary ingredient of a healthy relationship.

Think about it.

You cannot play it safe and get the best out of love. You have to sit at the table and trust that you have built a good enough hand to say, "All in". I have seen so many people get in relationships and remain in protection mode. Their goal is to avoid getting hurt. That is not how love works. Since you have been wise in your choice, you can operate in the strength of vulnerability. There are no guarantees, but there are many incredible possibilities. Invest yourself full into your relationship. All in.

Pray this together

God in heaven, you are our protector, and we are safe in your care. The scriptures say that perfect love casts out fear. We have chosen to commit to each other. We trust the decision we have made. We pray, therefore, for the strength and courage to be completely vulnerable with each other and to live and grow fully engaged in the relationship. We ask that no effect of a previous betrayal or any lingering insecurities stunt the potential of our relationship. We ask that you will keep us in perfect peace. We love each other and want the best relationship possible. Amen.

Do this together

Since your relationship is a safe place, engage in an activity with your companion that is out of your comfort. Broach a difficult subject. If you don't sing or dance, do so. Do something simple that requires you to trust in the security of your mate's commitment to you and the comfort of their love.

Notes

Real love is work. It's a joy and a pleasure, but it is work.

Think about it.

If a happy relationship was a car, please know that it would not have an automatic transmission, power steering, or cruise control. If it was a plane, it would not have an auto pilot setting. Real love is work. If you have the right person and you are blessed with the favor of God, your work will not be in vain. The work cannot be avoided though and your responsibilities cannot be transferred to anyone else, not even to God. If you put in the effort, you will get the results. If you don't, you won't.

Pray this together

God in heaven, you have done amazing things through your mighty power. Energize us so that we may consistently do the work required to make our relationship all it can be. I will not be a lazy or apathetic partner. I do not expect things to happen automatically. I know it will take constant effort, and my relationship is worth the work. Give us your grace as we strive to be excellent partners. We love each other and want the best relationship possible. Amen.

Do this together

Choose an area of your relationship that needs some work. Determine if you presently have the necessary tools. If you do, develop a plan and get to work.

Notes

Partners in a good relationship will complement and, when necessary supplement each other. They are two pieces of the same puzzle rather than two slices of the same pie.

(From my book, What You Say When You Say I Do)

Think about it.

The two of you do not have to be exactly alike to enjoy a healthy, happy, fulfilling relationship. Puzzle pieces are not identical. They are similar so that it is obvious they belong together, but they are shaped and cut so that they can connect, creating the full picture. If your personalities, philosophies, and approaches to life blend well together, you can add value and balance to each other. That is the stuff long lasting relationships are made of. Keep serving and sacrificing for each other and enjoy your differences.

Pray this together

God in heaven, you uniquely created us and we are fearfully and wonderfully made. We pray that we would be a great team and a solid unit. We want to learn and grow from each other, and use our individuality to enhance our relationship. Whenever there is conflict lead us to the place of agreement. When there is discord, help us to find harmony. We love each other and want the best relationship possible. Amen.

Do this together

This one is risky but can be worth it. Characterize your partner. Who are they? From your knowledge and perspective describe their personality, philosophies, and views on life. Discuss your perceptions. Clarify any inaccuracies.

Notes

You should always want to know if your partner is satisfied in the relationship. Sure, you can read signs, but periodically just ask.

Think about it.

In a relationship two people commit to meet each other's needs and expectations. You learn your partner's needs and wants and you use your individual ability and capacity to meet them. Your mate reciprocates. While your attempts to satisfy each other will be appreciated, you must actually achieve the goal the majority of the time. You don't want to be in the dark about where you stand. No news may not be good news. Occasionally just ask the question, "Is there anything you would like for me to do better".

Pray this together

God in heaven, we are grateful that you know us and allow us to know you. The scriptures clearly state what is required to please you. We pray to have similar clarity in our relationship with each other. I want my mate to be satisfied with our relationship and pleased with me. Their contentment is my priority. Help us to always speak the truth in love and receive it in the same. Strengthen our weaknesses and further leverage our strengths. We love each other and want the best relationship possible. Amen.

Do this together

Ask the question

Notes

Love should never be an assumption. It should always be a conclusion and a declaration. When you love someone, every day is show and tell

---

Think about it.

When it comes to love, the question, "Are you sure", always deserves a quick, definitive answer. Your words and your behavior will provide each of you with the security you need to be able to know that you are loved. Say it frequently and show your partner you love them through your common daily practices. Your everyday activity will justify your words. We draw conclusions based on the available information. Let your record speak for itself. Declare and display your love constantly so that you leave no room for doubt.

Pray this together

God in heaven, we are secure in your love. Your love is obvious. I pray that my words and deeds give my partner the security of knowing that my love is real and true. I know according to scripture that love is patient and kind. It is not arrogant, proud or rude. It is not easily irritable and keeps no record of wrong. We pray for your grace to love each other this way. We want to have the best relationship possible. Amen.

Do this together

Read 1 Corinthians 13: 4-7. These verses should be a part of the foundation of your relationship behavior. Each day this week read it from a different authorized translation. I would suggest NKJV, NIV, ESV, NLT, GNB, The Message, and AMP.

Notes

Why did you choose to become a couple? A long lasting, fulfilling relationship requires a good foundation. What is your why? Please know the answer, "Because we love each other" requires elaboration.

Think about it.

"What is your why" is an important question. Why something exists justifies its existence. You made a choice to be together. There were reasons for that decision, and hopefully they are good ones for they are the foundation of your relationship. Everything is built on that foundation. A strong "why" will motivate you to do your best and give you the determination to make it through the tough times.

Pray this together

God in heaven, you are the firm foundation. You are the reason we have life. It is our prayer that as we continue to build our relationship that you would always anchor us. Like the house built on the rock we want our relationship to stand the test of time. Don't allow us to crumble. Do not allow us sink. Hold us steady. We love each other and want the best relationship possible. Amen.

Do this together

Together write a foundational statement for your relationship detailing reasons why your relationship exists. It is your preamble of sorts. Keep it. You may never know when you may need to refer to it.

Notes

All touching should not be foreplay.

Think about it.

Touching should not just be a prelude to sex. It should also be done to maintain relationship intimacy. While generally speaking, men are more often prone to this behavioral pattern than women, it is important that there is an ample amount of affection in the relationship along with the sensuality.

Pray this together

God in heaven, it is amazing how the creator of the universe is still near to us. We pray that our love would be an affectionate one. We pray that our closeness would remain that our physical interaction would be an obvious indicator of the healthiness of our love. Lord, keep us attentive and drawn to each other so that we can always feel loved and cared for. We love each other and want the best relationship possible. Amen.

Do this together

Go somewhere and be the sickening couple. Hold hands. Engage in a lot of public displays of affection. Feed each other dessert. Take selfies. Watch the reactions. Have fun.

Notes

Make holidays special. Special does not always have to be expensive.

Think about it.

I was taught to never ruin or make crucial errors on holidays because there is always an anniversary of your mistake. I was also taught that holidays should be special. As a couple, you have 6 major holidays, your anniversary, each of your birthdays, Valentine's Day, Christmas and New Year's Eve. Every individual has particular preferences regarding these days, and each of you should know what your partner expects and enjoys. Plan, prepare and execute from the heart. Trust me it matters.

Pray this together

God in heaven, we praise who you are. We pray that our lives would be full of celebrations. Help us to always make each other feel special. We pray that our schedules would afford us the opportunity to be fully present on celebratory occasions, that finances would not be an issue, and that care and creativity would always be evident. We love each other and want to have the best relationship possible. Amen.

Do this together

Begin thinking about and planning for the next holiday celebration.

Notes

If you live a lie to avoid being alone, the real you is still single.

Think about it.

The Bible says that the first couple was naked and not ashamed, totally exposed to each other. That is the type of authenticity and transparency that is the hallmark of marriage. It is important when dating that people are honest about who they really are so that whoever chooses to love them makes that decision based on accurate information. If you suppress layers or large portions of yourself in order to conform to someone else's personal preferences, the real you remains without a companion. You are still alone.

Pray this together

God in heaven, you know all about us and choose to love us. We pray that in this relationship we would always have the space and comfort to be our true selves. We desire to be a great match for each other. We pray that our differences will not cause distance between us, and that we would appreciate the good and help each other improve the bad. As we grow and evolve as individuals remind us to continue to communicate about our personal changes so that we may grow together. We love each other and want the best relationship possible.

Do this together

Share something you like and something you dislike that your mate may not be aware of.

Notes

With is a strong word. "I'm with..." is the beginning of a powerful sentence. That is why Satan loves to separate, cause division, and orchestrate bad connections.

Think about it.

Awesome is one of the most overused words in the English vocabulary. For that reason, I do not use it much. Yet, being able to look at the person you love, respect, and admire and say to yourself, "She's with me" or "That's my man" is totally awesome. Being single has its advantages, but being a couples has so many more. So please don't allow your career, your kids or being in a big family steal your couple-ness from you. Set aside time just to be with each other. Enjoy the times when you get to buy two tickets to the show or request a table for two.

Pray this together

God in heaven thank you for blessing me with _____ (partner's name). Being with this amazing individual makes my life better and more fulfilling. Protect our relationship from anything that would divide us. Bless us to be as one. We love you each other and want the best relationship possible. Amen.

Notes

You are not responsible for your partner's happiness. A good relationship is when you connect with a happy person and help make them happier.

Think about it.

An individual's happiness is his or her own responsibility. That job cannot be outsourced. Too many unhappy people put undue pressure on their significant other to create, orchestrate or facilitate their personal happiness. Many people are disappointed in relationships because they have the unreal expectation that someone else is supposed to make them happy. Your partner is an enhancement to your life, a new ingredient, a variable or coefficient that adds increased value. Your relationship should take your life to the next level, but it is unfair to your partner if you are starting at zero.

Pray this together

God in heaven, you are the source of our joy and the strength for our lives. I pray that I would live my life in complete wholeness. Fix every broken place and heal every wound. Thank you for the value that _____ (partner's name) adds to my life. I confess that my happiness is not _____ (partner's name) responsibility. Help us to continue making each other happier. We love each other and want the best relationship possible. Amen.

Do this together

List the top 5 things that make you happy that are not connected to your relationship. List the top 5 reasons your relationship contributes to your happiness. Discuss each.

Notes

Don't let a bad seed be sown in good ground.

Think about it.

Every poisonous plant starts as a seed. Seeds are small but have amazing potential when planted and allowed to grow. Pay attention to weeds that are attempting to grow in your relationship. Be careful of the bad habits, experiences, or behaviors that become more frequent or stronger in intensity. There may come a time when something needs to eliminated, weeded out, because it is unhealthy and will keep your love from fully blossoming. Your relationship is meant to be a beautiful garden, but you must give it the proper attention to protect its beauty.

Pray this together

God in heaven, you are the giver of life. You bless us to live, grow and mature. Keep us from those things sent to choke our growth and stunt our development. We know we can't and shouldn't try to address every little thing, but help us to remain vigilant so that we may protect our relationship from people, spirits, personal traits and tendencies that could eventually destroy the beauty of our union. We love each other and want the best relationship possible.

Do this together

Discuss a negative personal trait that seems to run in your family. How will you protect your relationship from its effect?

Notes

Buying presents is not a substitute for constant absences. Invest the necessary time in your relationship. Presence makes a difference.

Think about it.

We live in a very superficial, materialistic culture. If you listen to hip hop, especially bad hip hop, you will hear women rapping about what their man buys or needs to be able to buy her. Men rap about how much money they can and will spend on women. Everybody claims to be able to make it rain. Nevertheless, for the mature companion, the most important thing you can spend is time. Sure, it is important to have the requisite funds to meet the needs of your relationship. Nice gifts are good, but being together is most important.

Pray this together

God in heaven, you are the creator of time and space. You give us the strength and the wisdom to make the most of every minute we have. We pray that we would always prioritize spending time together. I never want to neglect _____ (partner's name) in any way. We love each other and want to have the best relationship possible.

Do this together

Plan some extended time to be alone together.

Notes

Your significant other should not be made to feel insignificant.

Think about it.

You are a couple, but your life is comprised of many other relationships as well. Managing them all can be quite a juggling act. Each relationship has its own set of demands and obligations. Periodic conflict is inevitable. If you consistently make each other the top priority in life, you will both feel assured of your significance. When you are secure in your place and importance in the life of your partner, it will be easier to accept it when he or she must focus on something or someone else at a given time. When you are constantly reassured of your significance, situational sacrifices become easier to make.

Pray this together

God in heaven, you are the first and the last, the beginning and the end. You are the preeminent one in the universe. Thank you for the opportunity to love such a wonderful person. I pray that my love is always shown and my affection and appreciation are always evident. I pray that we remain assured and secure in our relationship in every situation. We love each other and want the best relationship possible. Amen.

Do this together

List the most important people in your life. Do any of them presently have any direct effect on your relationship?

Notes

As your partner evolves, those personal changes may affect your relationship. Continue getting to know your partner throughout the life of your relationship. You do not want to make assumptions or draw conclusions based on a previous version of the person you are with.

Think about it.

Let's face it. People change. Education, exposure, new experiences and aging are all factors that shape us as we evolve. No one stays the same nor should they. The beauty of being a couple is you get to grow together. As changes take place in your personality, views, likes and dislikes, be sure to communicate them to your mate. Your partner needs to be notified that an update is ready to be downloaded. If you do not give the update your mate continues to engage who you were rather than who you are.

Pray this together

God in heaven, you are the same today, yesterday and forevermore. You know our end from the beginning. We, on the other hand, must simply take life's journey. You bless us to live, change, grow, and mature. Thank you for someone so special with whom to take this journey. Again, we ask you to bless us to maintain healthy communication so that we never become strangers to each other. We pray that we would be both lovers and best friends.

Do this together

Periodically have "the state of my mate" conversations. This conversation is not about the relationship itself, the kids, the bills, etc. It is about what is going on with the person. This is the time to be reminded of who he or she is, note any changes, and download any updates.

Notes

Love is a decision and becomes a responsibility you have and a privilege you enjoy.

Think about it.

People do not usually analyze the phrase, "I love you" from the hearers point of view. While it is great to hear the words and it feels good to say them, those three words obligate you to a standard of treatment once you utter them. Once you establish how you want to be treated by someone who loves you, the right to say "I love you" then is something that is earned. Behavior substantiates the words spoken. Of course, there will be mistakes and failures along the way but too many people say those special three words without practicing them.

Pray this together

God in heaven, you prove your love to us every day. We have no doubts concerning your love for us. We recognize that love is what we do and not just what we say. We pray that we would always honor the words we have spoken remove you to each other. Our love is true. We want the best relationship possible.

Do this together

Listen to your favorite love song that talks about commitment. Discuss the messages in the lyrics. One of my favorites is "I Said I Love You" by R&B singer Babyface.

Notes

How can you make life easier for your mate?

Think about it.

Being in a couple allows you to share the load. Life is full of multiple responsibilities. Everybody could use a helping hand once in a while.

Pray this together

God in heaven, you lift our burdens and will not put more on us than we can bear. We pray that we would look out for each other. I want to lighten the load for my mate. We pray that we will always be attentive in order to see when either of us is overworked or overburdened. We love each other and want the best relationship possible.

Notes

Give each other a new reason to love you.   Let love keep growing.

Think about it.

If you follow the NBA as closely as I do you learn the tendencies of the players. The great ones make full use of the offseason. During their time off they add something to their game, a new shot, a new move, more muscle, more or less weight. Constant improvement is a hallmark of great players. You should keep improving as a companion. Perpetually make yourself a better mate. You both will enjoy the benefits.

Pray this together

God in heaven, you are the best thing that could ever happen to anyone. We pray that our love will keep growing. The better we are the better our love will be so we ask you to continue to work on us as individuals so that we may enhance our relationship. We love each other and want the best relationship possible. Amen.

Do this together

What is the next level of love you want to give? Think about it. Communicate it to each other. When you achieve it make sure you both acknowledge and celebrate the accomplishment.

Notes

25

Make sure that your relationship doesn't simply become a routine.

Think about it.

I know people who do not have a life. They have a routine. They have allowed their existence to become so mundane that they even bore themselves. It is easy to allow the same thing to happen to your relationship. Kids, work, school can dominate your daily schedule to the point that you simply survive each day. Couples can get in the habit of doing the same thing on a regular basis. Eventually it can be a relationship killer. Be creative and intermittently spontaneous. Try new things. Don't get bored.

Pray this together

God in heaven, you have created such variety in the universe. Absolutely nothing is exactly the same as anything else. We pray that we would never get overly settled in our relationship that we fail to incorporate new and different things. We do not want to be bored as a couple and ask that we both would always add to the creativity in our relationship.

Do this together

Do something you have never done together.

Notes

26

Consider it a relationship emergency when you do not communicate consistently and effectively. "We don't even talk anymore" is a problem that should not be ignored.

Think about it.

Good communication is one of the most important keys to a successful relationship. After one of you noticed the other, someone had to initiate some form of communication. You agreed to talk further. That is how you got know each other. Communication got your relationship started, and it should never be neglected. Talk. Listen. Text. Email. Video chat. Debate. Negotiate even argue. Consistent, healthy communication serves the same purpose lubrication does in machinery. It helps keep all the parts running smoothly.

Pray this together

God in heaven, you are the one who spoke the world into existence, and you also hear and answer our prayers. We understand the importance of healthy communication to our relationship. We pray that you would empower us to discipline ourselves to always keep the lines of communication open and to never use the silent treatment as a weapon. Help us to adequately understand and properly interpret and respond to each other's verbal and nonverbal messages. We pray that communication would always be a strength for us. We love each other and want the best relationship possible. Amen.

Do this together

Share with your partner a great conversation you've previously had with him or her. Talk about the reasons that particular conversation is so meaningful and memorable to you.

Notes

27

Feelings matter even though they can be temporary and even when they are not grounded in truth.

Think about it.

So much in a relationship is based on how a person is made to feel. The Meyers – Briggs Type Indicator differentiates between feeling and thinking persons. Individuals with a "thinking" personality may unnecessarily discount the role that feelings play in how a person processes reality and responds to life's occurrences. Whether you are a thinking or feeling person know that you cannot control or arbitrate how another person feels. The best you can do is appropriately respond and when possible, help them to process or clarify their feelings or support them as they cope with them.

Pray this together

God in heaven, you are not stoic and unfeeling. You feel joy, grief, and anger. You can be pleased and displeased. We are made in your image. We pray that we will always respect each other's feelings. Help us also to understand how to relate to each other when either of us experiences negative emotions. Keep us away from negative emotional extremes. We love each other and want the best relationship possible.

Do this together

What are your dominant emotional traits? How do you best manage yourself when you become overly emotional?

Notes

28

Risk being the first to reconcile.

Think about it.

Conflict is inevitable. There will be fights that cause hurt feelings. Sometimes you will cause pain. Other times you will be victimized. Regardless of who is at fault, it is best for the relationship that conflict is settled as quickly as possible to prevent any potential unnecessary damage. Don't wait. Be the first to extend the olive branch. Resolution is more important than who is right or who is wrong.

Pray this together

God in heaven, you gave your son, Jesus that the world might be reconciled to you. We pray for the humility and the courage to be peacemakers. During conflict give us the will to pursue healing and reconciliation above all else. Help us to always be gracious and kind. We love each other and desire the best relationship possible.

Do this together

Discuss who is better at making up. Is either of you terrible at it? Why?

Notes

29

Flirt with your partner often.

Think about it.

Your relationship began with some type of attraction. There were smiles, coy looks, little gifts, and public displays of affection. No matter how long you are together, do not rob your partner of the joy of being desired and pursued by you.

Pray this together

God in heaven, I simply pray that _____ will continue to be the object of my desire, and that I would show it regularly.

Do this together

You don't need any instructions from me at this time.

Notes

30

If you are going to actively love someone forever, you will eventually have to forgive them for something.

Think about it.

Prepare yourself for it. Get mentally and spiritually ready for it. Recognize it is a part of life and love. We all have to develop the capacity to forgive. Humans are flawed. We all fail from time to time. We make mistakes and poor choices. We disappoint the ones we love. Everybody does. Even you. Learn the discipline of forgiveness. Ask for it and accept it when needed. When you do not forgive, you allow your mind, emotions, and spirit to be held hostage. Free yourself, and also remember if you cannot forgive you cannot be forgiven.

Pray this together

God in heaven, you have forgiven us of so many things. You extend your mercy to us on a daily basis. We pray for the will to forgive. Help us to show each other grace and mercy when hurt or disappointed. We love each other and want the best relationship possible.

Do this together

Read Matthew 18:21-35 NLT

Notes

31

Be the president of your partner's fan club.

Think about it.

Everyone needs support and encouragement. How stimulating and motivating it is to have someone who truly believes in you. It gives you confidence to hear the one you love say, "I believe in you." True love is knowing that there is someone who is always in your corner. That person in your partner's corner should be you. Your significant other has value beyond their contribution to your relationship. Cheer each other on in your individual pursuits. Celebrate each other's accomplishments. Comfort each other in your failures and defeats. Give each other unrelenting support. Be your love's biggest fan.

Pray this together

God in heaven, there is none greater than you. You are worthy of all praise. I pray to always be counted on for encouragement, support and celebration. You have blessed me with a terrific person. I am committed to _____ (partner's name) individual success. I pray to consistently give my full support.

Do this together

Give each other a national holiday, a day of honor and celebration.

Notes

32

Find time to check in a couple of times during the work day.

Think about it.

The two of you are a tag team, a 1-2 punch. While your individuality is never erased or consumed by who you are as a couple, you are, nevertheless, a part of a unit. Members of an active unit stay in contact with each other so not to have to worry or wonder about each other and to be able to communicate any updates or occurrences that require action to be taken. Daily apply that logic to the treatment of your mate. Additionally, it is just nice to let your loved one know that you think about him or her throughout your day. Attention is a part of romance.

Pray this together

God in heaven, we desire to feel your presence always. It is essential for us to always know that you are there. We pray that our desire for each other and our discipline would remain strong. May we never feel alone, unnoticed, forgotten, or expendable. Though each day will be different, providing its own responsibilities, challenges and obligation, may we always make each other a priority. We love each either and want the best relationship possible. Amen.

Do this together

Discuss your desires and expectations relative to this subject. What makes you feel remembered? Is there a minimum amount of contact you prefer? Are there any constraints that prevent the amount of contact you would like to make?

Notes

33

You may not be able to repair what you did not break.

Think about it.

It is important to know if your mate is broken in an area and to what degree. Some people have been damaged by life experiences, and it can affect their relationships. Being hurt is different from being damaged. Damage results in diminished ability or capacity to perform or tolerate. As much as you love and serve your significant other there may be something broken that you cannot fix. You did not break it. It is not your fault. Help your loved one to undo the damage if possible. If not, work through it together so that it does not negatively affect your relationship.

Pray this together

God in heaven, it is your desire to make us whole. We pray for your healing in every broken place in our lives. Reveal those hidden things of which I may not be aware. I desire to be my best self and to live at full strength. Let nothing from my past cause a hindrance in the present. Protect our relationship from any collateral damage. We love each other and want the best relationship possible.

Do this together

When you're ready to do so without guilt, accusation, or hyper sensitivity discuss any brokenness you are aware of in yourself and how you deal with it. Does it affect your relationship in any way?

Notes

34

What do you mean when you say, "I love you"?

Think about it.

There are four basic types of love and friendship, family love, erotic love, and unconditional love. It is also possible to love the contribution someone makes to your life and confuse that with true love for him or her. So then, a declaration of love requires clarification and elaboration. Love is more than a set of feelings. Feelings can fool you. Be especially careful with erotic love. Those feelings can be very deceptive. It is possible to love the joy of it more than you love the person involved. Don't be fooled. Remember, words convey meaning. Say what you mean and mean what you say.

Pray this together

God in heaven, your love is definitive and obvious. We find comfort and safety in truth of your love. We love each other and pray that we continue to show that love in what we do and say. Our love is real, and pray that our actions would leave no doubt of that fact. Please continue to bless us. We want to have the best relationship possible.

Do this together

Write each other a love letter.

Notes

35

If it doesn't have to be a problem, then don't let it be.

Think about it.

Some conflicts can be avoided by simply letting them go. Choose not to overreact to negative stimuli. Things will happen. Try not to allow everything to be a big deal. Pursue peace. Get over things as quickly as possible. It will save emotional wear and tear on your relationship.

Pray this together

God in heaven, we seek your peace. Help to us to be slow to become angry and not easily offended. We know that little things can become big things if not managed properly. We pray that you would give us tolerance and temperance that we may avoid unnecessary conflict or strife. We love each other and want the best relationship possible.

Do this together

Discuss how each of you manage conflict. Is there a method that works best for your relationship? Is there a negative pattern that should be eliminated?

Notes

36

Always be your partner's plus 1?

Think about it.

Two is better than one, so they say. It should be. Your romantic partner should add value to your life, having a positive effect on you as an individual. You should make each other better. Both parties bring things to the table that enhance the other. I pray that you have chosen a quality individual to which to give your love and your life. God forbid that people are in love and in relationship with someone whose net effect on their life is negative or even neutral. Be a plus.

Pray this together

God in heaven, we are nothing without you. With you all things are possible. Thank you for this wonderful individual who makes me better. I pray that we would continue to grow, improve and excel as people and partners. Bless us to always be a blessing to each other. We love each other and want the best relationship possible.

Do this together

Make a list of the positive effects your partner has on you.

Notes

37

Where ever the grass is green, it is consistently being watered.

Think about it.

We can be tempted to compare the success of our relationship to that of someone else's. Unfortunately, some people while in a relationship, have been seduced into believing that they have found a better, more suitable, option for a mate. Things seem more natural, and they just seem to connect with the potential alternative option. Listen. I have said it before and will say it again. All relationships are work. Nothing is simply magical. Do the work for your love to last, be healthy and satisfying. If your lawn is green it is because of fertilizer, rain and your irrigation system. You and God partner to keep your grass green. Keep partnering with God in your relationship.

Pray this together

God in heaven, we trust that you will bless our relationship with your goodness. Keep us focused and faithful to the commitment we have made each other. We anticipate that there will be difficulties from time to time. Bless us to keep our attention on our love and not give in to the temptation to abandon our commitment to diligently work for the success of our union. We love each other and want the best relationship possible.

Do this together

Where are the "brown patches" in your relationship? Are there any aspects that could use a little extra water?

Notes

38

20 thoughts x 0 deeds = 0 deeds.

Think about it.

You have heard the old saying, "It's the thought that counts". That is not always true. It is easy to get caught in the trap of thinking of things you fail to execute. You thought about calling but didn't. You were going to do something special but failed to get around to it. You have frequently considered improving in an area but you have not taken the initiative. In order for your good deed to have the impact on your partner that is possible, the deed has to be done. Don't just think about it. Get it done.

Pray this together

God in heaven, give us great thoughts and ideas for our relationship. More importantly, we pray that we would put them into action to be a blessing to each other. We love each other and want the best relationship possible.

Do this together

Think about something you want to do for your mate then do it.

Notes

39

You can love deeply and not love well

Think about it.

Often we judge our love for others based on the depth of our feeling. We are quick to say we love from the bottom of our hearts. Yet, feelings can be strong and performance can be lackluster. I love music, but I don't sing well. I am fanatical about the game of basketball. I still try to play, and I attend many college and NBA games. Yet, I am an average player at best. I am not very good at what I deeply love. Do your best to love well. The quality of your love is as important as the depth of it. Make every effort to master what pleases your mate. Love your partner on the level he or she requires, and if those requirements are minimal, love your mate beyond his or her wildest imagination.

Pray this together

God in heaven, you do all things well. I want to be an excellent companion. Bless me so that what I feel in my heart is consistently seen in my action. Give me a clear understanding of _____ (partner's name) needs and desires and empower me to fulfill them. Bless us to succeed in our efforts to please each other. We love each other and want the best relationship possible.

Do this together

Choose an area you want to improve. Develop a plan. Discuss your plan with your partner.

Notes

40

If your partner is not meeting your needs and expectations, make them aware of it. If you pretend to be satisfied you rob each of you of possible improvement.

Think about it.

If your relationship were to eventually fail because you were silent while dissatisfied or hurting, then you would be an accessory to its murder. We can allow love to die a slow death when because of a misguided effort to avoid conflict, we refuse to confront issues that become lethal to the relationship. Your partner cannot work on a problem he or she does not know exists. Speak up. Pray and work on it together. Get some relationship coaching or therapy if necessary. If you do not face it, you cannot fix it. Do not suffer in silence.

Pray this together

God in heaven, you confront us with our sins and transgressions that we might repent and be redeemed. Lord, empower us to be comfortable and confident enough to come to each other with any need that we may have. We pray that we would always be able to trust the strength of our love enough to take the necessary action to make us better. Since it is our desire to please each other, prepare us to always be open to evaluation or any necessary critique without becoming offended. We love each other and want the best relationship possible.

Do this together

Make a pact that you won't pretend to be happy or satisfied. Work with each other and give each other the chance and the space to improve anything that may be lacking.

Notes

41

Habitually keep your word. It will make you trustworthy and dependable.

Think about it.

"Just do what you say you are going to do". Those words were spoken to me on an occasion when I had committed more than I delivered. Words create expectations and initiate an agreement and a trust between you and the hearer. Once you speak, your words become your representative. People depend on them to be as certain as your physical presence. When you fail to keep your word it potentially disrupts the plans of another. If this happens with any degree of regularity, you establish a level of uncertainty to anything to which you are involved and your dependability is called into question. So, don't overextend yourself. Try not to be inordinately forgetful. Do not over promise and under deliver, and of course don't be a liar.

Pray this together

God in heaven, your word is forever true. We depend on it for our daily lives. We pray to be careful with our words so that our dependability cannot be called into question. I always want _____ (partner's name) to be able count on me. We are a tag team. We love each other and want the best relationship possible.

Do this together

Does either of you have a tendency to overextend or overpromise? At times your desire can be greater than your capacity to perform. How can you be more realistic so that you may be more dependable?

Notes

42

Before adding something to your life (children, extra job, school, business pursuits, etc.), consider the effect it will have on your relationship and plan for any necessary adjustments.

Think about it.

We all manage multiple priorities. The decisions we make in one area of our life affects others. Life is like a jigsaw puzzle or very important game of Jenga. Unless you are at retirement age, you will probably keep adding new variables to your life as you pursue your personal passions, professional goals and ambitions. Consider the potential the impact your other priorities will have on your relationship. Be intentional with your decisions. Don't just roll the dice and hope for the best. Choosing the right timing and performing a cost-benefit analysis are very important for people with multi-faceted lives.

Pray this together

God in heaven, we ask you to lead us. Direct our decisions and our choices. You know what we need and when we need it. You know how the pieces of our lives are purposed to fit together. Give us your wisdom and guide us with your Spirit. We love each other and want the best relationship possible.

Do this together

What do you personally want to accomplish during the next 12 to 24 months? Are you considering new financial, travel, or time commitments? Will any of your new pursuits affect the present state of your relationship?

Notes

_____

_____

_____

_____

_____

_____

_____

_____

/43

Don't take away your partner's ability to give you the benefit of the doubt.

Think about it.

No one is perfect. We all make mistakes and poor choices. Good intentions do not always yield a positive result, and at times we fail while giving it our all. Yet, if we are known for being truthful, maintaining our integrity, doing the right thing, and getting things done, we remain believable when things seem suspect, and we will engender confidence when others are apprehensive about the outcome of a given situation. Your partner's ability to give you the benefit of the doubt helps him or her maintain stability and inner peace. To lose it hurts you both.

Pray this together

God in heaven, we know we can trust you without any hesitation. Your track record speaks for itself. Your word is true. We pray that we would live our lives in such a way that we remain trustworthy and that our confidence in each other would remain strong. Credibility with each other is important, and we want to maintain it. Please don't allow any hidden or unknown personal insecurities to affect how we relate to each other. We love each other and want the best relationship possible. Amen.

Do this together

Discuss any personal insecurities that affect your ability to trust others. Have a conversation about any personality quirks that could over time affect your credibility i.e. forgetfulness.

Notes

44

When is the last time you discussed your personal wishes, dreams, or ambitions? As a couple, you are vested in each other's dreams.

Think about it.

There are two individuals within the couple, each with their own dreams and ambitions. Some desires you had prior to beginning your relationship. Others you have developed since the two of you have been together. It is important that your relationship provides the space for you to pursue those things while continuing to live in concert with each other. Let there be no conflict between who you want to be, what you want to become, and who you want to be with. Allow your dreams to coexist, and help each other achieve them.

Pray this together

God in heaven, you are able to do exceedingly, abundantly, above all we can ask or imagine. You know the plans you have for our lives. We desire to be everything you have purposed us to be. We realize that we cannot have it all at the same time so lead us and keep us in the center of your will and moving at your pace. I want _____ (partner's name) to live a life of total fulfillment. I commit to assist, support and even sacrifice so that we can make our dreams come true together. We love each other and want the best relationship possible.

Do this together

Have the discussion and talk about your plans. Discuss timing and how you can assist each other. Work out any conflicts with your ambitions and your relationship.

Notes

45

Have fun on a regular basis.

Think about it.

Do I really have to say much about this one? The more you laugh and do things you enjoy together the healthier your relationship will be. Make time for entertainment, adventure, and celebration. Life is stressful and relationships are work. You need some playtime on a consistent basis. Remember how important recess was to you in elementary school? Your relationship needs recess.

Pray this together

God in heaven, your word says that laugher is like medicine. We pray that laughter would always be a large part of our relationship. You have also placed so many things in the world for us to enjoy and we desire to take advantage of as many as possible. Give us the discipline to take the time, and where necessary, the resources to experience as many as possible. We love each other and want the best relationship possible.

Do this together

Go have some fun.

Notes

46

Some conflicts may not be solved quickly. When there is a lingering problem, don't let it bleed into the rest of the relationship. Protect the good that remains from the bad you are experiencing.

Think about it.

The ability to compartmentalize is a key attribute during conflict. Emotions can be unpredictable when there is contention so it is important to practice self-control. Try not to let one thing ruin your perspective on everything else. We tend to let the negative dictate our feelings and our relationship interaction. Why not find the positive and let it dominate your mood and how you relate to your partner? And by all means, please do not abandon or neglect your mate in a time of need because you happen to be angry with him or her at the time.

Pray this together

God in heaven, you are patient and longsuffering. We pray to be the same with each other. We recognize there will be times when conflict is not quickly resolved. During those times help us to remember that we have a good relationship that is simply going through a difficult period. Cause us to never allow the area of conflict to dominate our feelings or our view of our lives together. Help us to always support each other and treat each other with honor and respect even while angry. We love each other and want the best relationship possible.

Do this together

Make a list of what you love about your mate and your relationship. Keep it. Refer to it during those extended times of discouragement or despair.

Notes

47

Your relationship most likely will not fulfill every emotional and social need you have. Try not to put undue pressure on your relationship by letting it be all you have or deciding it is all that you need.

Think about it.

I have seen so many people put far too much stress on their relationship. They require their mate to be their everything. What a burden that is. Yes, romantic partnership involves meeting the needs and expectations of another, but some people have too many needs and their expectations are frankly too high. It is important to have additional interests and social networks so as not to require your partner to be your all. Do not to kill your relationship by suffocating your partner or live your life unsatisfied because you depend on your significant other for total fulfilment.

Pray this together

God in heaven, only in you do we find total sufficiency. You alone have all power. We thank you for our relationship. It means the world to us. Today we pray for all of our other family and social connections. We ask that you would bless them that they might be positive contributors to our lives. We understand life is a puzzle with various pieces. Bless all the pieces of our lives to fit together perfectly. We love each other and want the best relationship possible.

Do this together

Think about the other aspects of your life. What relationships need nurturing? What are your favorite hobbies? Incorporate "me time" into your schedule.

Notes

48

Be consistently loving, kind, and caring. Neglect and ambivalence are relationship termites, and no one wants a mean partner.

Think about it.

Maintenance! Maintenance! Maintenance! We tend to ignore it with cars, our health, our teeth, and unfortunately with our relationships. And we do it to the peril of them all. Cars break down. Medical and dental conditions develop unnecessarily, and relationships can die a slow death when we underestimate the importance of routine maintenance. I repeat. Be consistently loving, kind, and caring. Going the extra mile on special occasions is wonderful, but what is the normal vibe of your relationship? Give your partner consistent attention. Show love and care regularly. Let there be no doubt.

Pray this together

God in heaven, your love is better than life. You bless us with your benefits daily. We pray that we would be consistent in the little things, regular attention, frequent acts of kindness, and loving support. We know that we possess the power to make each other's day. Help us to use that power to bless each other and continue to build our relationship. We love each other and want the best possible relationship.

Do this together

Make a list of the "little things" you like to receive from your mate. Exchange lists with your partner.

Notes

/49

Make sure the relationship continues to nurture the individuals within the couple.

Think about it.

The two of you have become one in love and life. If you are married you are one in God. Yet, you are still individual persons with your own dreams, desires, and the need for continued development. The old cliché says, "There is no I in team". I say there is a "me" in every "we". Real love is when you care about your mate as a person as well as his or her contribution to you and the relationship. No one should have to become a zero in order for the two of you to become one.

Pray this together

God in heaven, every individual is fearfully and wonderfully made. Thank you for bringing someone in my life who values me. I want to be all that you have purposed me to be. I have someone who loves me as I am but loves me enough to help me reach my potential. Use our relationship as an instrument to make us our best selves. We love each other and want the best relationship possible.

Do this together

Communicate to your partner what your prayers, hopes and dreams for them as an individual are.

Notes

50

Keep a little fantasy in your reality.

Think about it.

Whether it is Cinderella and Prince Charming at the ball, Richard Gere and Julia Roberts in the movie, Pretty Woman, or Eddie Murphy and Shari Headley in the movie, Coming to America, fantasy will always be popular. I know life is real though, and relationships are work. Every day you make essential decisions, pay actual bills, handle true stress and love a real person. As you live your lives together do not try to live in a fantasy world, but make some dreams come true, have some unforgettable experiences that are made for the movies.

Pray this together

God in heaven, you are able to bless us beyond our wildest dreams. As we live our lives together we pray that you not only make life fulfilling but please make it incredible. We love each other and want the best relationship possible.

Do this together

Describe for each other what a fairytale-like evening date or experience would be.

Notes

51

A good partner will require you to be a better person.

___

Think about it.

"I want somebody to love me as I am but love me enough to not let me stay like this". I heard a woman speak those words in the early 1990's and they have stuck with me ever since. What a sentiment that is. If you have a partner who loves you and challenges you to be your best you, remain open to his or her assistance. The president of your fan club should have the space to give you constructive criticism when necessary along with helping you grow and improve so that you become your best self.

Pray this together

God in heaven, thank you for blessing me with someone who adds to my life and with whom I can trust throughout my different stages of development. I desire to be the best person I can be so as to be a great mate and amazing partner for _____ (partner's name). Bless us to be each other's safe place to grow. Do not let pride and ego get in the way. We love each other and want the best relationship possible.

Do this together

Discuss a character trait you are presently working to improve.

Notes

52

You made it through the year. What are your highlights?

Think about it.

You committed yourselves to spend this time together for an entire year for the benefit of your relationship. You did it! Congratulations! I believe your relationship is better and stronger. You have had some helpful discussions and more importantly prayed some powerful prayers. I'm sure there are some things that stand out now, but you have also sown seeds that will bear fruit in the future. Keep holding each other's hand as you move forward in life and love.

Pray this together

God in heaven, our future is in your hands. We pledge to continue to do the work necessary for a great relationship. We ask you to do the rest. Please bless our life together and our love. We want to show the world that true love and a fulfilling relationship can still be reality. With your help, we can do just that. We ask for your grace, mercy, and blessed favor to be with us always. We love each other and want the best relationship possible. Amen.

Do this together

Discuss the growth in your relationship.

Notes

Made in the USA
Monee, IL
27 January 2022

89971958R10063